Middle Age
SPREAD

Other For Better or For Worse® Collections

Retrospectives

Middle Age
SPREAD

A For Better or For Worse® Collection by Lynn Johnston

Andrews McMeel
Publishing

Kansas City

98 99 00 01 02 BAH 10 9 8 7 6 5 4 3 2 1

ISBN: 0-8362-6822-9

Library of Congress Catalog Card Number: 98-85337

GUESS WHAT, DAWN—I'VE FINALLY DECIDED WHAT I'M GONNA DO WITH MY CHRISTMAS MONEY!

I'M GONNA GET CONTACT LENSES! I'M GOING DOWN TO THE OPTOMETRIST'S OFFICE WITH MY MOM TOMORROW, AN' GET A PRESCRIPTION!

COOL, LIZ! YOU'RE GONNA LOOK, LIKE TOTALLY DIFFERENT!

I DUNNO, MAN... I NEVER LIKED THE IDEA OF PUTTIN' SOME FOREIGN OBJECT INTO MY EYES!!

YOUR PRESCRIPTION WILL BE READY IN A WEEK, ELIZABETH!

A WHOLE WEEK?

I THINK THIS IS PRETTY EXCITING! WE DIDN'T WANT YOU TO HAVE CONTACT LENSES, BUT I THINK YOU'RE OLD ENOUGH NOW TO LOOK AFTER THEM!

DUH!

IT'S NICE BEING WITH YOU TODAY, HONEY! I'M GLAD YOU DON'T MIND BEING SEEN DOWNTOWN WITH YOUR MOTHER!

NAH!

...ALL MY FRIENDS HANG OUT AT THE MALL.

SHAKE, SHAKE

SHAKE SHAKE SHAKE

I PUT SALT ON THE STAIRS LIKE YOU ASKED ME TO DADDY... BUT IT SURE TOOK A LONG TIME!

6

9

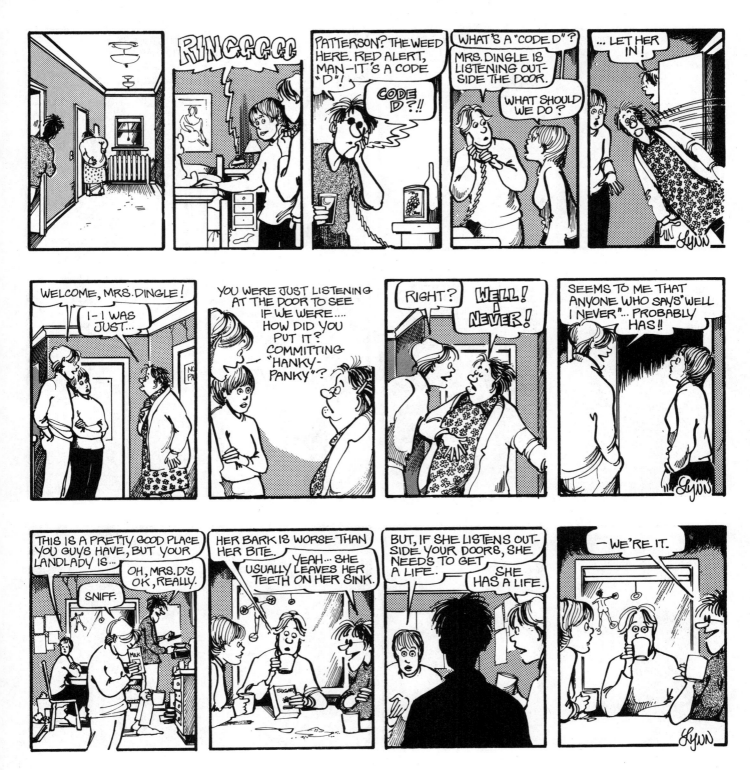

I DUNNO, GUYS, I'D RATHER LIVE IN RESIDENCE THAN HAVE A LANDLADY WHO WANTS TO KNOW EVERYTHING I'M DOING!

RESIDENCE?! DEANNA, THE REZ IS CRAZY! PEOPLE PARTY, THERE'S CONSTANT NOISE, JUNK ALL OVER THE PLACE—AN' YOU'VE GOT ABSOLUTELY NO PRIVACY!!

HOW CAN YOU STUDY IN A PLACE LIKE THAT?!!

BLAST! Lynn

WHAT DO YOU KNOW ABOUT YOUR LANDLADY, MICHAEL?

MRS. DINGLE?

SHE WAS A WAR BRIDE, CAME TO CANADA AT THE AGE OF 18, WORKED AS A SEAMSTRESS, HAD 3 CHILDREN. TWO DIED OF POLIO AND THE THIRD LIVES IN OHIO.

SHE'S WIDOWED NOW AND RENTS ROOMS IN HER HOUSE TO STUDENTS.

DOES SHE NEED THE MONEY?

NOPE... SHE NEEDS THE FUN!

Lynn

I DON'T KNOW, MIKE. MRS. DINGLE DOESN'T APPEAR TO HAVE MUCH OF A SENSE OF HUMOR.

SHE SEEMS TO HAVE A PERPETUALLY SOUR LOOK ON HER FACE.

YEAH...

AND I HAVEN'T BEEN ABLE TO FIGURE OUT WHY.

Lynn

FILL 'ER UP, MRS. P?

I'LL DO IT, TRACEY!

YOU SHOULDN'T BE WORKING OUTSIDE ON A DAY LIKE THIS!

I FEEL FINE. REALLY!

THE BABY KICKS A LOT NOW. IN FACT, IT'S SO ACTIVE THAT SOMETIMES I CAN'T SLEEP!

... MUST BE A BOY!

YOU AND GORDON SHOULD CALL US BY OUR FIRST NAMES NOW, TRACEY— AFTER ALL, WE ARE INVESTORS HERE!

I KNOW.

AND YOU AND I ARE BOTH MOTHERS NOW— THAT GIVES US EVEN MORE IN COMMON!

I GUESS IT DOES!

I'VE TAKEN EVERY BOOK OUT OF THE LIBRARY ON BIRTH AND BABY CARE, AN' GORD AND I HAVE STARTED CLASSES, SO I GUESS WE ARE STARTING TO FEEL LIKE PARENTS, BUT....

ELLY, WHAT'S IT _REALLY_ LIKE?!!

WHAT'S HAVING A BABY LIKE? WELL, EVERYONE'S EXPERIENCE IS DIFFERENT, TRACEY—AND THE FIRST TIME IS ALWAYS SUCH A BIG ADVENTURE!!!

BUT PEOPLE TELL YOU SUCH HORROR STORIES!

DON'T LISTEN! YOU'LL BE FINE. YOU'RE STRONG AND HEALTHY, YOU HAVE A LOYAL PARTNER...

I KNOW.

I GUESS WHAT I'M AFRAID OF — IS THE PAIN... IT IS PAINFUL, ISN'T IT.

UH HUH-BUT IT BECOMES UNIMPORTANT WHEN THE TIME COMES.

WHY?

YOU DON'T THINK ABOUT PAIN WHEN YOU'RE PRODUCING A MIRACLE!

Panel 1: HEY, MRS.P.—I HEAR YOU AN' THE DOC ARE TAKING A WEEK OR 2 OFF!—GONNA DRIVE DOWN THE COAST? / THAT'S THE PLAN, GORDON.

Panel 2: I'LL MAKE SURE YOUR CAR WILL GET YOU THERE AN' BACK—BUT SHE'S IN PRETTY GOOD SHAPE THESE DAYS!

Panel 3: STILL, A COUPLE'A WEEKS—ESPECIALLY ON UNFAMILIAR ROADS—REALLY TEST A VEHICLE!

Panel 4: NOT TO MENTION A MARRIAGE.

Panel 5: SORRY I'M SO LATE GETTING HOME, GIRLS—I HAD TO GET GAS, I HAD TO GET GROCERIES... / PANT PUFF

Panel 6: HERE, PUT THESE AWAY, LIZ, GET APRIL TO SET THE TABLE AND I'LL PUT THE OVEN ON! / IT'S OK, MOM.

Panel 7: —DAD'S AT A DINNER MEETING DOWNTOWN, AN' WE ATE. / YOU MEAN I DON'T HAVE TO RUSH ANYMORE?—I HAVE SOME TIME?!!

Panel 8: WEIRD. WHENEVER THAT HAPPENS, YOU'D THINK SHE GOT A GIFT OR SOMETHING!

Panel 9: WOW! I HAVE TIME TO MYSELF THIS EVENING—FOR THE FIRST TIME IN AGES! / MENDING PILE

Panel 10: I CAN DO ANYTHING I WANT! HAVE A BATH, READ A BOOK, CALL A FRIEND...

Panel 11: I COULD WATCH A MOVIE OR DO MY NAILS.....I HAVEN'T DONE **THAT** FOR A LONG TIME!

Panel 12: YOU KNOW, JOHN—IT'S AMAZING HOW GOOD IT FEELS TO HAVE AN EVENING **FREE** FOR A CHANGE!!

20

WHAT DID YOU DO IN SCHOOL TODAY, ELIZABETH?

OH... STUFF.

YOU'RE IN LOVE WITH ANTHONY, AREN'T YOU! BECKY SAW YOU KISSING AT THE MALL!

AN' GUESS WHAT! MOM AN' DAD KNOW TOO, 'CAUSE MRS. POTTS SAW YOU KISSING UNDER HER STREETLAMP THE OTHER NIGHT!

WHY DOESN'T EVERYONE JUST MIND THEIR OWN BUSINESS?!

WHY DON'T YOU JUST STOP KISSING?!

Lynn

KNOW WHAT, LIZ? WHEN MOM AN' DAD GO ON THEIR HOLIDAY, THEY'RE GETTIN' A BABYSITTER FOR US!

WHAT?!

BUT I ALWAYS STAY WITH DAWN AN' YOU ALWAYS STAY WITH BECKY WHEN THEY'RE AWAY!!

NOT THIS TIME.

DAD SAYS THAT AN EMPTY HOUSE ISN'T A GOOD THING— I GUESS HE DOESN'T TRUST PEOPLE.

YOU MEAN, HE DOESN'T TRUST **ME**!!

Lynn

MOM, WHAT'S THIS ABOUT US BEING BABYSAT WHILE YOU GO ON HOLIDAY?

YOU'RE NOT BEING "BABYSAT," HONEY.

SALLY FROM THE CLINIC IS GOING TO STAY HERE WHILE THEY PAINT HER APARTMENT —IT'S A PERFECT SITUATION.

WE NEVER HAD TO DO THIS BEFORE! IT'S 'CAUSE I'M DATING ANTHONY NOW, ISN'T IT! YOU DON'T TRUST US IN AN EMPTY HOUSE— DO YOU!!!

OF COURSE WE TRUST YOU, HONEY!

... WE JUST DON'T TRUST THE CIRCUMSTANCES.

Lynn

DON'T YOU THINK WE'RE BEING A LITTLE OVER-PROTECTIVE OF ELIZABETH, JOHN? SHE COULD STAY WITH DAWN WHILE WE'RE AWAY.

WE'RE DOING THE RIGHT THING, EL. WE'RE NOT LEAVING THE HOUSE EMPTY FOR TWO STARSTRUCK KIDS TO PLAY IN.

NO, SIR! - I WANT ELIZABETH TO STAY INNOCENT AND NAIVE FOR AS LONG AS POSSIBLE.

GASP, KISSSSS FEEL.... GROPE OOOOH... NUZZLE... GROANNNNNN

YOU'VE MET SALLY BEFORE, GIRLS - SHE WORKS AT THE CLINIC!

YEAH.

HI!

SHE'S GOING TO STAY IN THE REC ROOM WHILE WE'RE AWAY - BECAUSE HER APARTMENT IS BEING PAINTED, AND SHE NEEDS A PLACE TO STAY!

DADDY, HOW LONG WILL YOU BE GONE? CAN I COME? WILL YOU BE HOME SOON? I DON'T WANT YOU TO GO!

NOW I KNOW WHY THEY ALWAYS SAY "GUILT WEIGHS HEAVY!"

ON THE ROAD AT LAST! - I'VE BEEN LOOKING FORWARD TO THIS TRIP, EL!

...JUST YOU AND ME AND TWO WEEKS OF FREEDOM!!

AND SALLY'S A NICE GIRL. I KNOW THAT SHE AND ELIZABETH WILL GET ALONG JUST FINE!

Panel 1: DON'T YOU JUST LOVE THE HISTORY AND THE ARCHITECTURE IN THESE SOUTHERN TOWNS, EL!

Panel 2: —THE WAY THE OLD CHURCHES, HOMES AND COURTHOUSES HAVE BEEN PRESERVED..

Panel 3: YES SIR, I COULD LIVE DOWN HERE, COULDN'T YOU?!! / I DON'T THINK SO.

Panel 4: —IT WOULD MEAN WE'D HAVE TO **STOP** SOMEWHERE!!!

Panel 5: AHA! JACKSONVILLE! SEE? I TOLD YOU WE'D MAKE IT TO FLORIDA — AND WE DID!! / JACKSONVILLE NEXT 4 EXITS

Panel 6: THIS IS FLORIDA, EL! AT HOME, THERE'S FREEZING RAIN — AND WE'RE IN **FLORIDA!**

Panel 7: WE MADE IT IN LESS THAN A WEEK — ISN'T THAT GREAT? / UH HUH... JUST IN TIME!

Panel 8: JUST IN TIME FOR WHAT? / ...TO TURN AROUND AND GO BACK.

Panel 9: THE PROBLEM WITH YOU AND I GOING ON A DRIVING HOLIDAY, JOHN, IS THAT YOU HAVE AN <u>AGENDA</u> AND I DON'T! — YOU ALWAYS HAVE TO <u>GET</u> SOMEWHERE!!

Panel 10: I LIKE TO TAKE MY TIME, MEANDER SLOWLY, LOOKING AT LITTLE SHOPS, STOPPING AT LOVELY LITTLE RESTAURANTS...

Panel 11: —WE COME TO A NICE LITTLE TOWN — AND YOU WANT TO BLAST RIGHT THROUGH!

Panel 12: THAT'S 'CAUSE I DON'T <u>WANT</u> TO MEANDER SLOWLY, LOOKING AT LITTLE SHOPS, AND STOPPING AT LOVELY LITTLE RESTAURANTS.

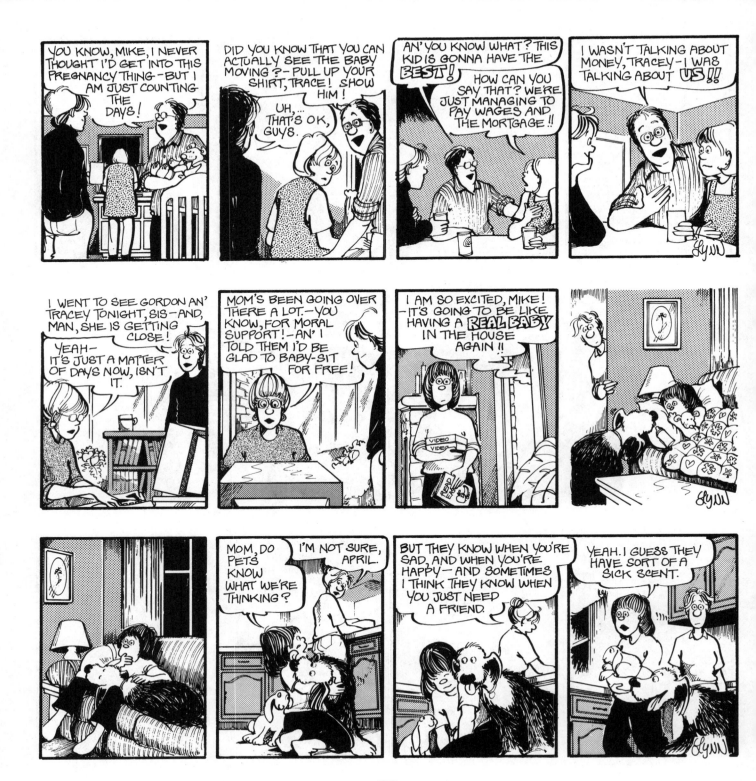

Panel 1: We're calling him Paul, after Gordon's grandfather. / He's a beautiful baby, Tracey.

Panel 2: How are you feeling? / Well, I'm walking better, but sitting down is a challenge —and I'm trying to nurse him, Elly...

Panel 3: Was the hospital staff helpful? / Oh, sure.... and my mother and Gord's mother, and everyone around has given us volumes of advice!

Panel 4: So, why is it that we still don't know what we're doing!!

Panel 5: I know how you feel Tracey. I was the same when Michael was born. I thought that if I read all the books and took all the advice, that being a mom would be easy!

Panel 6: But, after 3 kids, I realized that each one comes into your home a stranger—and you have to get to know and trust each other. / WAH!

Panel 7: Your baby is trying to figure you out—as much as you and Gordon are trying to understand him!! / I never thought of it that way.

Panel 8: ...I sure hope he likes us.

Panel 9: Were you visiting the new family? / I took Tracey a casserole, and some other things I thought they could use.

Panel 10: Strange... I'd forgotten how to hold a new baby! —I'd forgotten how floppy and tiny and helpless they are!

Panel 11: And you forget how uncomfortable it is to sit down afterward, how awkward nursing is at first—and how much work there is to do! ...I can't believe that you can forget what it's like to have a brand-new baby!

Panel 12: ...I guess that's why we keep having more.

IT'S FINISHED, JOHN — WHAT DO YOU THINK?

NEW CARPET, NEW DRAPES, NEW FURNITURE, NEW WALLPAPER — I'VE FINALLY FINISHED THE "SPARE ROOM"!

I DON'T KNOW HOW SHE CAN CALL THIS THE "SPARE" ROOM...

... IT'S JUST COST US A BUNDLE!!

MICHAEL'S ROOM LOOKS LIKE A HOTEL ROOM NOW, ELIZABETH.

YEAH... BUT THAT'S WHAT MOM WANTED.

AND MICHAEL SAID HE DIDN'T MIND. I MEAN, HE'S ONLY HOME A FEW TIMES A YEAR NOW, AN' FOR THE SUMMER.

SO WHAT'S GONNA HAPPEN WHEN YOU GO AWAY TO SCHOOL?

MORE E-MAIL?

IT'S FROM LIZ. MY ROOM IS NOW AN OFFICIAL "GUEST ROOM."

YEAH. AS SOON AS I MOVED OUT, MY MOM TURNED MY ROOM INTO "OFFICE SPACE" WITH A FOLD-OUT COUCH.

WELL, LIKE WE SAID BEFORE, MAN — YOU CAN'T KEEP THINGS THE SAME. STUFF CHANGES.

AN' THAT'S OK!

— AS LONG AS THE PEOPLE DON'T!!

I'VE GOT 2 MORE EXAMS TO DO, DEANNA. ONE, I THINK I'LL DO OK ON ... THE OTHER IS MULTIPLE CHOICE.

THEY LOVE TO PUT "TRICK QUESTIONS" ON MULTIPLE CHOICE. YOU EITHER KNOW THE STUFF OR YOU DON'T ... SO WHAT'S THE POINT IN CONFUSING EVERYONE WITH "TRICK QUESTIONS"?

MY ROOMMATE SAID THE LAST TIME SHE GOT A GOOD MARK WAS WITH THE E.M.M.M. ANSWERING SYSTEM!

... EENIE, MEENIE MINEY, MOE!

HEY, WEED! YOU LOOK WEIRDED OUT! -TOUGH EXAM TODAY?

NO...

I GOT TOP MARKS FOR MY PHOTO ESSAY ON ADDICTION. THEY'RE PUTTING MY WORK ON DISPLAY IN THE LIBRARY. I MIGHT EVEN GET IT PUBLISHED.

WHAT?

CONGRATULATIONS, MAN! THAT IS SO COOL! - WHAT DID YOUR PARENTS SAY?

NOT MUCH.

THEY THINK THAT PHOTO-JOURNALISM IS A HOBBY.

YOU HAVEN'T MET MY FOLKS YET, MIKE.

YEAH. I ALWAYS WONDERED WHY WE NEVER WENT TO YOUR PLACE.

SPLORK!

WELL, MY DAD AN' I DON'T EXACTLY AGREE ON SOME STUFF. HE'S AN IMPORTER. HE HAS A HUGE BUSINESS AND HE WANTS ME TO GO INTO IT WITH HIM.

HE WANTS ME TO TAKE LAW OR BUSINESS OR ACCOUNTING - BUT THAT'S NOT ME!

RIGHT! YOU GOTTA GO WHERE YOUR HEART TAKES YOU. DO WHAT YOU WANT TO DO!

THAT'S WHAT HE SAID.

... THEN I CAN GO INTO LAW OR BUSINESS OR ACCOUNTING.

ELIZABETH, WHAT'S HAPPENING? WE USED TO DO ALL KINDS OF STUFF TOGETHER—AN' NOW, ALL YOU WANNA DO IS BE WITH ANTHONY!

YOU WERE SO JEALOUS WHEN I STARTED TO HANG OUT WITH CANDACE AND SHAWNA-MARIE—AN', NOW YOU HARDLY TALK TO **ME** ANYMORE!

I KNOW WHAT IT'S LIKE TO BE IN LOVE, BUT YOU'RE CUTTING YOURSELF OFF FROM ALL YOUR FRIENDS. ...LIZ?

LOVE ISN'T JUST BLIND... IT'S DEAF, TOO!!

CHECK IT OUT, LIZ! I JUST PASSED MY DRIVING TEST!

ANTHONY, THAT IS SO COOL!

YEAH! ME AN' SOME FRIENDS ARE GONNA GO CRUISE 'ROUND THE USED CAR LOTS, AN' SEE WHAT'S THERE.

CAN I COME?

WELL, I'D SAY YEAH, BUT THERE'S NOT ENOUGH ROOM IN FRANK'S CAR... AN' BESIDES, IT'S, YOU KNOW—A "GUY" THING.

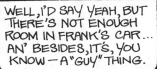

WHAT'S THE MATTER WITH ELIZABETH?

I DUNNO, BUT SHE SAYS IT'S A "GIRL" THING.

SNIFF... HE DOESN'T CALL ME ANYMORE. HE SPENDS EVERY NIGHT WITH THE GUYS. ALL THEY TALK ABOUT IS CARS!

WE KNOW HOW YOU FEEL, LIZ.

EVERY GIRL GOES THROUGH THIS.

REALLY?

WHEN A GUY GETS HIS LICENSE, HE IGNORES HIS GIRLFRIEND, AN' ALL HE CAN THINK ABOUT IS CARS!!—THEY'RE LIKE THIS GIANT **SEX** SYMBOL!

BUT, WHO ARE THEY TRYING TO IMPRESS?

US!

Panel 1: SO I PASSED EVERYTHING. DIDN'T GET THE GREATEST MARKS IN THE WORLD, BUT GOOD ENOUGH TO GET IN AGAIN.

ME, TOO.

Panel 2: YOU'RE READY TO GO, ARE YOU? WELL, DON'T EXPECT TO RENT THIS PLACE AGAIN IN THE FALL, UNLESS I GET A LITTLE SOMETHING IN ADVANCE.

Panel 3: (silent embrace)

Panel 4: ...USUALLY, I TAKE CASH.

Panel 5: YOU WANNA GO OVER TO THE REZ AN' SAY GOODBYE TO DEANNA?

SHE LEFT YESTERDAY.

Panel 6: IT'S WEIRD, ISN'T IT, WEED. FOR 8 MONTHS, WE LIVE IN DORMS AN' RENTED ROOMS, STUDYING... SOMETIMES LOVING, SOMETIMES HATING SCHOOL.

Panel 7: BUT IT'S LIKE HOME, SOMEHOW. LIKE, WE'RE LEAVING HOME TO **GO** HOME. WE'RE SUSPENDED BETWEEN TWO REALITIES.

YEAH!...

Panel 8: —ONE'S A ROCK, THE OTHER'S A HARD PLACE.

Panel 9: SO, I'M GUESSING THAT YOURS IS NOT "HOME SWEET HOME."

I DON'T FIT INTO THE MOLD, MIKE.

Panel 10: I HAVE ONE SISTER, A NURSE WHO IS HAPPILY MARRIED, SO MY DAD IS LOOKING AT ME TO TAKE OVER HIS BUSINESS.

Panel 11: BUT I'M A PHOTOGRAPHER! AN' I WANNA TAKE CHANCES —JUMP OUTTA AIRPLANES, CLIMB INTO VOLCANOES, COVER A WAR—LIVE ON THE EDGE!

Panel 12: WEED.... HOW COME YOU DON'T HAVE A STEADY GIRLFRIEND?

...TOO DANGEROUS.

WHERE ARE YOU OFF TO?

DRIVING LESSONS!

I'M GONNA BE 16 ON THE 28TH, SO I BOOKED MY TEST FOR THE SAME DAY...AN' I'M GONNA PASS, TOO!!

WOW...APRIL'S TOO BIG TO CARRY, LIZ IS DRIVING, MOM AN' DAD ARE GOING GRAY.....HAS **ANYTHING** STAYED THE SAME SINCE I CAME HOME LAST YEAR?

JUST LOOK AT YOU!-ALL COVERED IN GRASS STAINS AND TRACKING DIRT INTO THE HOUSE!

...THERE'S NOTHING LIKE A GOOD ROMP WITH YOUR DOG TO MAKE YOU FEEL LIKE A KID AGAIN!!

WHERE ARE YOU GOING, MICHAEL?

DOWN TO CHECK ON MY JOB. I GOTTA START TOMORROW.

BUT YOU JUST **GOT** HERE!

WELL— WHY DON'T YOU COME WITH ME?

WE'LL STOP AT THE ICE CREAM CIRCUS AND GET A CONE, OK?

BONUS!

ELLY...THE STRANGEST THINGS MAKE YOU CRY!

Panel 1: HERE WE ARE, APRIL! WHAT WOULD YOU LIKE?
A KRAZY KONE!

Panel 2: WELL! IS THIS YOUR LITTLE GIRL?
NO! SHE'S MY SISTER.

Panel 3: OH, REALLY?
HONEST! HE REALLY IS MY BROTHER!

Panel 4: HE WAS JUST BORN FASTER THAN I WAS!!

Panel 5: SO MICHAEL'S HOME FROM UNIVERSITY!
YEAH.
I WISH SCHOOL WAS OUT FOR US, TOO.

Panel 6: SPEAKING OF SCHOOL... I DID GREAT WITH MY DRIVING LESSON LAST NIGHT, AN' MY INSTRUCTOR SAYS I'LL PASS — NO PROBLEM!

Panel 7: WELL, IN GENERAL, I THINK THAT WOMEN ARE MUCH BETTER DRIVERS THAN MEN.
I TOTALLY AGREE.

Panel 8: FOR ONE THING, WE'RE NOT AS EASILY DISTRACTED.

Panel 9: IT'S BEEN GREAT HANGING OUT WITH YOU, LIZ! WE THOUGHT WE'D LOST YOU FOR SURE!

Panel 10: YEAH—IT'S NOT GOOD TO BE SO CRAZY ABOUT A GUY THAT YOU LOSE ALL YOUR FRIENDS!

Panel 11: THIS IS A TOTALLY COOL PLACE! HOWCOME YOU WANTED TO MEET US AT CLUB SODA?

Panel 12: ... I THOUGHT ANTHONY MIGHT BE HERE.

Panel 1:
WHAT'S WITH YOU, LIZ?
WELL, YOU HARDLY SPEAK TO ME IN SCHOOL... YOU HAVEN'T CALLED ME FOR A WEEK!

Panel 2:
I'M SORRY, BUT THE GUYS AN' I HAVE BEEN CHECKING OUT CARS, AN'...
ANTHONY— YOU'RE SPENDING MORE TIME WITH "THE GUYS" THAN YOU ARE WITH ME!

Panel 3:
HEY, IT'S NOT THAT I DON'T LOVE YOU, LIZ.
I KNOW... IT'S JUST THAT LATELY, I'VE BEEN TAKING A BACK SEAT!

Panel 4:
—THAT'S WHAT I HAD IN MIND.

Panel 5:
IT'S BEEN AMAZING, LIZ! FRANK HAS TAKEN ME TO ABOUT 10 DEALERSHIPS!

Panel 6:
AN' WE'VE BEEN TESTING OUT SOME TOTALLY HOT VEHICLES! YOU KNOW, MEAN, FAST, SEXY... GREAT STEREOS!

Panel 7:
BUT, ANTHONY, SHOULDN'T YOU BE LOOKING FOR A CAR YOU CAN AFFORD?
WE'VE DONE THAT ALREADY...

Panel 8:
BUT NONE OF THEM GO.

Panel 9:
SO YOUR FRIEND ANTHONY IS LOOKING FOR A CAR, IS HE? I SHOULD TAKE HIM OVER TO GORDON'S FOR SOME GOOD ADVICE.
COOL!

Panel 10:
I'VE BEEN MEANING TO ASK HIM TO LOOK AROUND FOR US, TOO!
TELL HIM WE WANT A RED ONE!

Panel 11:
WHEN YOU BUY A SECONDHAND CAR, APRIL, YOU DON'T HAVE MUCH CHOICE WHEN IT COMES TO COLOR.

Panel 12:
... EXCEPT RUST.

Panel 1: WE'RE GOING DOWN TO GORDON'S GARAGE, MIKE—WANNA COME? / NO THANKS, POP.

Panel 2: I SAW GORD AN' TRACEY AN' THE NEW BABY YESTERDAY—AN' I WANNA GET TO WORK A BIT EARLY.

Panel 3: MOM, DUNCAN'S DAD IS HERE TO TAKE US TO THE PARK. I'M REALLY SORRY, BUT THAT MEANS YOU'RE GONNA BE LEFT HERE ALL *ALONE*!

Panel 4:

Panel 5: IT'S A REAL COINCIDENCE YOU SHOWED UP TODAY, DOC. I'VE GOT A LITTLE CAR HERE THAT A GUY WANTS ME TO SELL FOR HIM.

Panel 6: SHE'S A '93, GOOD BODY CONDITION, GOOD MOTOR... / HOW ARE YOU DOING, TRACEY?

Panel 7: OK, LIZ—IT'S JUST THAT NOW THAT WE HAVE THE BABY, I CAN'T GET ANYTHING DONE, AND IT'S DRIVING ME NUTS! / WHAT ABOUT HIRING A SITTER?

Panel 8: YOU KNOW—I WAS HOPING YOU'D ASK!!!

Panel 9: SO, WHAT DO YOU THINK, ANTHONY? / IT'S A GOOD CAR, DR. PATTERSON, BUT I REALLY CAN'T AFFORD ANYTHING RIGHT NOW.

Panel 10: I DON'T EVEN HAVE A SUMMER JOB YET.

Panel 11: BESIDES... IT'S THE KINDA THING YOU REALLY HAFTA THINK THROUGH. YOU CAN'T JUST GO FOR THE FIRST CAR YOU SEE!! / YOU'RE ABSOLUTELY RIGHT.

Panel 12: ...I WONDER WHAT HE WANTS FOR IT!!

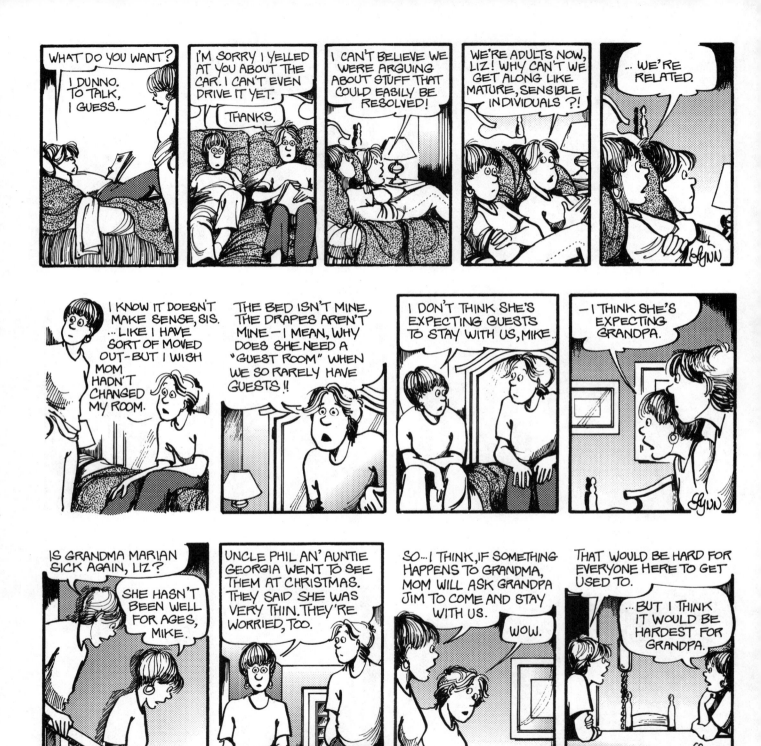

Panel 1: WHEN DO YOU AND APRIL LEAVE FOR VANCOUVER? — ON FRIDAY.

Panel 2: WE HAVE FAMILY THERE. APRIL WILL BE STAYING WITH MY COUSIN AND HIS KIDS, AND I'LL STAY WITH DAD.

Panel 3: MOM'S SCHEDULED FOR SURGERY NEXT TUESDAY MORNING. — IS SHE SCARED? — NO...

Panel 4: ...BUT EVERYONE **ELSE** IS!!

Panel 5: MOM—UNCLE PHIL'S ON THE PHONE!

Panel 6: I WISH I COULD COME WITH YOU, SIS. PROMISE YOU'LL CALL AS SOON AS YOU KNOW HOW MOM IS? — OF COURSE I WILL. — GOOD—AND, I'LL TRY TO GET THERE AS SOON AS I CAN!

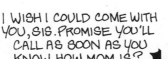

Panel 7: I FEEL SO GUILTY. THEY'RE ONLY A 5-HOUR FLIGHT AWAY—AND WE RARELY SEE THEM.

Panel 8: SIS, WE'RE ONLY A 5-HOUR **DRIVE** AWAY... AND WE RARELY SEE <u>EACH OTHER</u>!

Panel 9 (bottom row):

I HOPE MY MOM WILL BE OK. THEY SAY THERE'S A CHANCE SHE'LL RECOVER.

MY FOLKS HAVE ALWAYS BEEN SO INDEPENDENT. I CAN'T SEE EITHER OF THEM WANTING TO MOVE TO A SENIORS' HOME. — SAME WITH MINE.

WHAT WERE YOU TALKING ABOUT? — HOW DIFFICULT IT BECOMES WHEN YOUR PARENTS GET OLD.

YEAH. THAT IS A REAL PROBLEM, ALRIGHT.

MIKE AN' I WERE WONDERING WHAT WE WERE GONNA DO WITH **YOU** GUYS!!

ELLY! DAD! GRAMPA!

ARRIVALS

YOUR UNCLE JAY AND AUNT MOLLY ARE EXPECTING US FOR SUPPER. RON, CHERYL AND THE KIDS CAN'T WAIT TO HAVE APRIL STAY WITH THEM...

YOUR MOTHER'S SISTERS ARE HERE FROM THE ISLAND — AND OUR FRIENDS HAVE BEEN DOING EVERYTHING EVER SINCE YOUR MOM WENT INTO THE HOSPITAL.

OH, ELLY, I'M SO GLAD YOU'RE HERE! — I DIDN'T WANT TO GO THROUGH THIS ALONE!

Lynn

THEY'VE BEEN OPERATING FOR 3 HOURS, NOW. HOW LONG IS IT GOING TO TAKE?

I DON'T KNOW, DAD. I THINK IT DEPENDS ON WHAT THEY FIND.

HEART BYPASS SURGERY IS COMMON NOW — AND, MOM IS AN AMAZING WOMAN.

BUT, SHE'S SO FRAIL.

SHE'LL SURVIVE, DAD. I KNOW SHE WILL. THE MOST DIFFICULT PART OF THIS IS GOING TO BE THE RECOVERY.

THE MOST DIFFICULT PART OF THIS IS GOING TO BE THE WAITING.

Lynn

CAN WE SEE HER NOW?

YES, BUT NOT FOR LONG.

THE OPERATION WAS A BIG ONE. WE HAD TO DO A TRIPLE BYPASS.

IS SHE GOING TO BE ALL RIGHT, DR. STANLEY?

WE'LL KNOW MORE TOMORROW, JIM. — IT'S TOO BAD WE COULDN'T JUST GIVE HER ANOTHER HEART.

... SHE'S HAD MINE FOR OVER 40 YEARS.

Lynn

Panel 1:
HI, AUNTIE MARIAN!

HELLO, MY DARLINGS.

Panel 2:
WE BROUGHT YOU SOME CARDS WE MADE OUR-SELFS—AN' SOME FLOWERS!

THEY'RE LOVELY.

Panel 3:
DID YOU HAVE A REALLY BIG OPERATION, GRAMMA?

YES. THEY HAD TO OPEN MY CHEST FROM HERE TO HERE.

Panel 4:
EWW! GROSS!!

...CAN I SEE?!

Panel 5:
WHAT ARE WE GONNA DO, SIS?

I DON'T KNOW, PHIL. MOM WILL NEED SOMEONE TO COME AND TAKE CARE OF HER ON A REGULAR BASIS, IF SHE AND DAD ARE GOING TO KEEP LIVING AT HOME.

Panel 6:
THERE ARE SEVERAL ORGANIZATIONS THAT PROVIDE THESE SERVICES.

YES—BUT YOU KNOW HOW INDE-PENDENT OUR FOLKS ARE!

Panel 7:
I FEEL SO GUILTY, ELLY. I WISH WE HADN'T MOVED SO FAR AWAY.—**WE'RE** THE ONES WHO SHOULD BE TAKING CARE OF THEM!!

Panel 8:
PHIL... COULD YOU GIVE MOM A BATH?

WHERE'S THE PHONE BOOK?

Panel 9:
MOM, HOW MUCH LONGER DO WE HAFTA STAY HERE?

A FEW MORE DAYS, APRIL.

Panel 10:
WE'RE JUST WAITING FOR THE HOME-CARE SERVICES TO CALL US, AND FOR GRANDMA TO BE DISCHARGED FROM THE HOSPITAL.

Panel 11:
BAM!

LOOK, GRANT—ROMEO'S FOLLOWING ME!

CATS DO THAT, APRIL. HE'S PRETENDING YOU'RE PREY...

SEE? HE'S WATCHIN' YOUR FEET!—AN' WHEN HE GETS A CHANCE, HE'LL...

POUNCE

SEE?—IT'S CALLED "STALKING!"

—IT USED TO BE A "SOCK!"

KITTY TREATS

CRAK CRUNCH

Panel 1: SO, WHAT ARE YOU GONNA DO NOW THAT YOU'RE A FREE WOMAN?

WHAT DO YOU MEAN?

Panel 2: WELL, YOU'VE GOT A SUMMER JOB, A BOY-FRIEND, YOUR DRIVER'S LICENSE — LIFE IS **HAPPENING** FOR YOU, SIS!

Panel 3: NO MORE TAKING THE BUS DOWN TO THE MALL AN' HANGING AROUND THE FOOD COURT! — THE WORLD IS YOURS!!

YEAH!

Panel 4: WHAT DID YOU DO THE FIRST DAY YOU GOT YOUR LICENSE, MIKE?

UH... GORD AN' I DROVE DOWN TO THE MALL AN' HUNG AROUND THE FOOD COURT.

Panel 5: YOU GOT YOUR DRIVER'S LICENSE? ELIZABETH, I'M SO PROUD OF YOU!!

FIRST TRY, TOO!!

Panel 6: I'M SORRY I CAN'T BE THERE TO GIVE YOU A BIG HUG AND CONGRAT-ULATE YOU IN PERSON, HONEY!

Panel 7: THAT'S OK, MOM. I KNOW THAT GRANDMA AN' GRAMPA NEED YOU RIGHT NOW.

Panel 8: BESIDES, THE LONGER YOU STAY AWAY — THE LONGER I CAN HAVE YOUR CAR!!

Panel 9: LOOK, MOM! I CAN WIGGLE MY FRONT TOOF WIF MY TONGUE!

Panel 10: IF IT COMES OUT WHILE WE'RE AWAY FROM HOME, WILL THE TOOTH FAIRY KNOW WHERE TO FIND ME?

OF COURSE SHE WILL!

Panel 11: WHAT DO TOOTH FAIRIES DO WITH THE TEETH THEY COLLECT?

I'M NOT SURE, APRIL.

...WHY DON'T YOU ASK YOUR GRANDPA?

Panel 12: SNOZZ

Panel 1:
IS GRAMMA STILL REST-
ING, GRAMPA?

YES — BUT I SHOULD
GET HER UP.

Panel 2:
MARIAN? THE DOCTOR
SAYS YOU NEED TO WALK
A LITTLE MORE, IF YOU
CAN. DO YOU FEEL UP TO
IT?

I'LL TRY.

Panel 3:
(no dialogue)

Panel 4:
YOU SEE? WE CAN GET
ALONG JUST FINE
WITHOUT
YOU !!

Panel 5:
I HAVE TO GO SOON, EL. I
HAVE SUMMER STUDENTS
TO TEACH — AND GEORGIA
HAS SOME PLANS...

I KNOW,
PHIL. I
HAVE TO
GO HOME,
TOO.

Panel 6:
BUT MOM'S OUT OF THE
HOSPITAL NOW AND DAD'S
MANAGING WELL.

Panel 7:
AND WITH THE HOMECARE
WORKERS COMING, I'M
SURE THEY'LL BE FINE
WITHOUT US.

Panel 8:
DARN. I WAS SURE I'D
TURNED THAT BURNER
OFF !!

Panel 9:
PHIL? ELLY? YOUR
MOM AND I THINK
YOU SHOULD GO
HOME TO YOUR
FAMILIES.

Panel 10:
WE HAVE FAMILY
HERE AND GOOD
FRIENDS — THEY'LL
TAKE CARE OF US
IF ANYTHING
HAPPENS.

Panel 11:
IT WAS SO GOOD OF
YOU TO COME... AND
YOU CAN SEE
THAT I'M FINE
NOW
!

Panel 12:
YOU HAVE LIVES OF
YOUR OWN TO LEAD,
THINGS OF YOUR
OWN TO DO — GO
HOME, AND ENJOY
THE REST OF THE
SUMMER !

Panel 13:
... AND DON'T
WORRY ABOUT
US !!

LITTLE APRIL, ELLY AND PHIL ARE GOING HOME TOMORROW.

I KNOW. WE'LL MISS THEM.

IT WAS GOOD THEY CAME. I HAVE TO TELL YOU, MARIAN —WHEN YOU HAD YOUR SURGERY, I WAS TERRIFIED—I DON'T KNOW WHAT I'D DO WITHOUT YOU.

...YOU'D SMOKE TOO MUCH, WASH YOUR CLOTHES TOO LITTLE, AND NEVER EAT YOUR VEGETABLES.

I'M SO GLAD YOU CAME BACK.

I'M SO GLAD YOU STILL NEED ME.

I HOPE MOM AN' DAD WILL BE OK, SIS.

ME TOO.

BEEP!

I LIKED BEING IN VANCOUVER, UNCLE PHIL! I HAD FUN WITH JAIME AN' GRANT. CAN WE SEE THEM AGAIN SOMETIME?—DID YOU KNOW THAT THEIR CAT, ROMEO, CHASES BUTTERFLIES?

BIP BIP BIP

KIDS!—THEY DON'T UNDERSTAND WHEN SOMETHING'S SERIOUS!

BEEP

YOU JUST **THINK** WE DON'T UNDERSTAND.

MENOPAUSE- MUCH ADO ABOUT SOMETHING

DR. LELAND MCCOSHUN

BIP

DO WE HAFTA SAY GOODBYE, UNCLE PHIL?

YES WE DO, KIDDO. I HAVE A LONG DRIVE HOME.

FLT.

IT'S BEEN GOOD TO SEE YOU AGAIN, SIS! TOO BAD IT WAS MOM'S ILLNESS THAT HAD TO BRING US ALL TOGETHER.

YEAH!

WE SHOULD SEE EACH OTHER MORE OFTEN!

I KNOW. IT'S JUST THAT WE'VE BOTH BEEN SO CRAZY WITH WORK THAT, BEFORE YOU KNOW IT, THE TIME HAS JUST **FLOWN** BY!!

...I THOUGHT TIME ONLY FLEW WHEN YOU WERE HAVING **FUN!**

SHLLURFFTttt

SO WE'RE DOING A LAST-MINUTE, DOWN-TO-THE-WIRE CLEANUP BEFORE MOM COMES HOME, ARE WE?

APRIL, YOU'VE ACTUALLY GROWN SINCE I SAW YOU LAST!!

AN' MY FRONT TOOF CAME OUT, TOO!

DID YOU CHANGE YOUR HAIR COLOR, ELIZABETH?

JUST A BIT.

WELL, AFTER A FEW WEEKS OF YOU 3 BEING ON YOUR OWN, I KNOW YOU'LL HAVE A LOT TO TELL ME!

YEAH!

FIRST OFF, WE DIDN'T BREAK MUCH.

DID YOU MISS ME?

OF COURSE I MISSED YOU!

DID YOU MISS ME?

EVERY DAY!

COME ON, EDGAR...THIS IS GETTING **YUCKY!**

MMM! — DID YOU MISS ME, EDDY?

SLORUP!

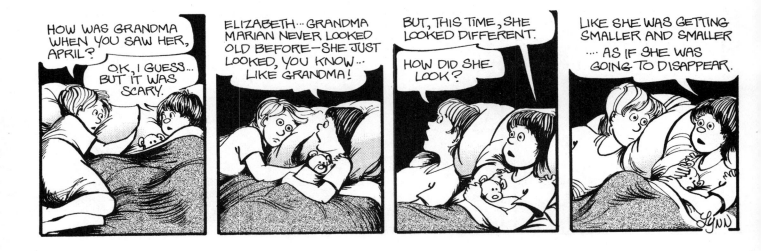

Panel 1: HOW WAS GRANDMA WHEN YOU SAW HER, APRIL?

O.K, I GUESS... BUT IT WAS SCARY.

Panel 2: ELIZABETH... GRANDMA MARIAN NEVER LOOKED OLD BEFORE—SHE JUST LOOKED, YOU KNOW... LIKE GRANDMA!

Panel 3: BUT, THIS TIME, SHE LOOKED DIFFERENT.

HOW DID SHE LOOK?

Panel 4: LIKE SHE WAS GETTING SMALLER AND SMALLER .... AS IF SHE WAS GOING TO DISAPPEAR.

IT'S A CRAZY TIME FOR ME RIGHT NOW, CONNIE. MY PARENTS NEED ME ON ONE SIDE OF THE COUNTRY—

AND, MY FAMILY NEEDS ME ON THE OTHER!—I'VE GOT KIDS AT HOME, AND ONE AWAY....

AT A TIME IN MY LIFE WHEN I THOUGHT THINGS WOULD BE EASIER, I'M STRETCHED TO THE LIMIT!

I KNOW, EL...

IT'S WHAT YOU CALL YOUR "MIDDLE AGE SPREAD."

HEY, YOU NEVER TOLD ME THAT BEN WAS GOING TO PARIS, LAWRENCE.

I KNOW. I KEPT HOPING IT WASN'T TRUE.

BUT HE GOT A SCHOLARSHIP TO STUDY PIANO AT LE CONSERVATOIRE - SO HOW CAN I HOLD HIM BACK?

I'M PROUD AND HAPPY FOR HIM - BUT I'M GONNA MISS HIM SO MUCH, IT'S GOING TO HURT LIKE NOTHING I'VE EVER FELT BEFORE!

MAN, I CAN'T BELIEVE I'M ACTUALLY TELLING YOU THIS!!

AND WOULD YOU BELIEVE THAT I ACTUALLY UNDERSTAND?!!

BEN ISN'T LEAVING FOREVER, LAWRENCE. BESIDES - YOU HAVE TO BE PREPARED TO FEEL PAIN IF YOU'RE GONNA FALL IN LOVE.... THAT'S PART OF THE PROCESS!

YOU BOTH LET DOWN ALL OF YOUR DEFENCES, YOU ALLOW SOMEONE TO ENTER YOUR HEART, - AND YOU TAKE THE RISK OF LOSING EACH OTHER.

BUT IT'S THE JOY OF HAVING HAD THAT TIME TOGETHER THAT MAKES IT ALL WORTHWHILE! - IT'S THE LAUGHS, THE MEMORIES - AND ALL THE GOOD STUFF YOU'VE SHARED - THAT MAKE FALLING IN LOVE.... WORTH THAT RISK!!

LET IT BE KNOWN THAT THIS SPEECH COMES FROM A GUY WHO'S IN A "HAPPENING" RELATIONSHIP.

I GOTTA SAY THAT YOU AND YOUR FAMILY HAVE BEEN GREAT TO ME, MIKE.

WHAT ARE YOU TALKING AB'OUT?

MY BEING GAY HAS NEVER CHANGED OUR FRIENDSHIP. YOU'VE NEVER TREATED ME LIKE I WAS EVIL OR WEIRD OR ANYTHING.

HECK, WE'VE KNOWN YOU SINCE WE WERE LITTLE KIDS!!

BUT I HAVE TO TELL YOU, LAWRENCE. THERE IS ONE THING ABOUT YOUR LIFESTYLE THAT HAS BOTHERED ALL OF US FOR A LONG TIME.

REALLY? WHAT'S THAT?!!

.... YOU DON'T EAT YOUR CRUSTS.

THERE ARE SO MANY SUPER STORES COMING INTO THIS CITY, CONNIE—PEOPLE AREN'T SHOPPING DOWNTOWN ANYMORE.

IT'S CHANGING OUR WHOLE AMBIANCE... EVERYONE GOES TO THE MALLS, AND THE SMALL, PRIVATE SHOPS CAN'T KEEP UP!

I WISH MORE PEOPLE WOULD SUPPORT THE DOWNTOWN.

I DO, ELLY.—I SHOP ON THE MAIN STREET ALL THE TIME!

...IF IT'S NOT RAINING OR SNOWING... AND I CAN FIND A GOOD PARKING SPOT!!

IT'S NOT JUST THE LOCAL DOWNTOWN, CONNIE... EVERYTHING IS CHANGING!!

DAILY, YOU HEAR ABOUT SOME NEW TECHNOLOGY THAT WILL REVOLUTIONIZE INDUSTRY, MARKETING, EDUCATION, ART!

WE ARE LIVING IN THE MOST DYNAMIC AND INNOVATIVE TIME IN HISTORY!

I KNOW.

AND TO SOME 6-YEAR-OLD TWIRP.... THESE ARE GOING TO BE THE "GOOD OLD DAYS"!

WHAT'S EDGAR EATING, APRIL?

A TOAD.

CHOMP SMAK CHEW

WHAT?!!!

DADDY RAN OVER IT BY MISTAKE THE OTHER DAY. IT WAS PRETTY FLAT.... I GUESS ED DIDN'T NOTICE 'TIL IT STARTED TO SMELL BAD.

BLEAH! BLEACH! GIMME THAT THING!! AAUGH! BLEAH!

WEIRD... I THOUGHT SHE BELIEVED IN RECYCLING!

I HAD A LOT OF TIME TO THINK WHILE I WAS HOME THIS SUMMER, WEED.

3 OF THE GUYS I KNOW ALREADY HAVE JOBS... OR AT LEAST A GOOD IDEA ABOUT WHAT THEY'RE GONNA DO!

WHAT ARE YOU SAYING?

I DON'T KNOW IF I WANT TO BE A JOURNALIST— WHAT I REALLY WANT TO BE IS A SERIOUS WRITER!

JOURNALISTS ARE SERIOUS WRITERS, MIKE... AND, SOMETIMES, THEY GET PAID!

MR. WEEDER, COULD YOU TELL US SOMETHING ABOUT THIS PHOTOGRAPH?

THIS IS A YOUNG WOMAN WHO LIVES WITH HER 2 CHILDREN IN AN OLD VAN, BEHIND A RESTAURANT.

SHE CLEANS THE RESTAURANT EVERY NIGHT IN EXCHANGE FOR FOOD AND THE USE OF THEIR WASHROOM AND ELECTRICITY.

WHAT POVERTY-STRICKEN COUNTRY DOES SHE LIVE IN?

THIS ONE.

EACH ONE OF THESE PHOTOGRAPHS HAS SUCH AN AMAZING STORY BEHIND IT, WEED.

I KNOW.

I TITLED THEM ALL, BUT I NEVER HAD TIME TO WRITE UP MY NOTES!

I'LL DO IT, MAN!—PEOPLE SHOULD KNOW MORE ABOUT WHAT GOES ON IN THIS CITY!—I MEAN, THESE AREN'T JUST FLAT IMAGES—THEY'RE REAL!

—AND YOU SAY YOU DON'T WANNA BE A JOURNALIST!!

 MMMMM

FOR ME, JOHN...THIS TIME OF YEAR IS PURE HEAVEN!

 THE SMELL, THE COLORS, THE MARKETS, THE COOL, FRESH WINDS.

 OF ALL THE SEASONS—I THINK I LIKE THIS THE BEST.

 WE'VE SEEN A LOT OF AUTUMNS TOGETHER, HAVEN'T WE, EL. MORE THAN 20!

 I GUESS YOU COULD SAY WE'RE IN THE "AUTUMN OF OUR LIVES!"

 THAT'S A NICE ANALOGY, JOHN – COMPARING A LONG-LASTING RELATIONSHIP TO THIS TIME OF YEAR. YEAH...

 FOR ONE THING, THERE'S FEWER BUGS.